THE MOST

Wonderful

TIME OF THE YEAR

Written & Compiled by Ruth Austin · Designed by Jill Labieniec

*This is a place where we are with the ones
we love most, gathered around a table, celebrating,
amidst the red, green, and gold, the feast laid
before us, and the presents... And we remember
the memories that make up who we are.*

KATE BONACINI

THE HOLIDAYS ARE A BRIGHT AND MAGICAL TIME.
A time apart—like no other—when for a few shining, glimmering
moments we put aside our normal routines. The holly hanging
in the hall, the mistletoe overhead, and the feast on the table fill
us with coziness and joy. And as we gather our friends and
family close to us, as we celebrate and laugh and unwind, the
whole world just seems to sparkle a little bit more.

Wherever you are this holiday, and whatever your plans, turn
the page, take a moment, and welcome the festive season—
the most wonderful time of the year.

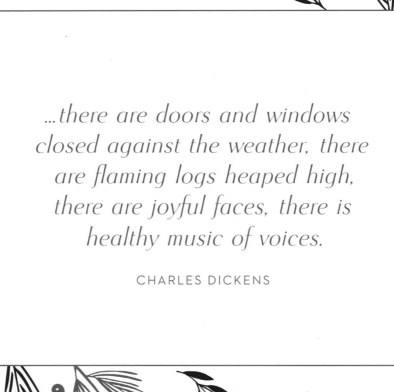

...there are doors and windows closed against the weather, there are flaming logs heaped high, there are joyful faces, there is healthy music of voices.

CHARLES DICKENS

...fellowship, feasting, giving and receiving,

A TIME OF GOOD CHEER...

| W. J. TUCKER |

Our hearts are happy

AND OUR LOVED ONES
ARE CLOSE BY.

*Let the sound of laughter brighten
each corner of this house...*

MARILYN HUNTMAN GIESE

...oh, the fun of arriving at a friend's house and feeling the immediate spark which tells you that you are going to have a good time.

MARK HAMPTON

It's in the noise of celebration

THAT WE EXPERIENCE JOY...

| TRISH KASPAR |

*...the sun looks down on nothing half so good
as a household laughing together over a meal...*

| C. S. LEWIS |

We celebrate the past year

AND LOOK TOWARDS
THE YEAR AHEAD.

...may you know many

blessings in the company of

loved ones and true friends.

CORRINE DE WINTER

*We didn't realize we were
making memories, we just knew
we were having fun.*

UNKNOWN

We were together, and that's all that mattered.

| WHITNEY WOODY |

We remember the love

WE HAVE FOR
EACH OTHER.

A home is not a place; it's a feeling.

| HELEN LA PENTA |

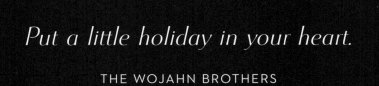

Put a little holiday in your heart.

THE WOJAHN BROTHERS

Sometimes the smallest family rituals create

THE RICHEST MEMORIES.

| NICOLE WISE |

People and packages, secrets and song, holly wreath at the door, colored lights as we drive along... snowflakes glowing through window panes, and a lovely feeling inside.

| MARGARET HILLERT |

We notice tiny marvels and

DISCOVER LITTLE
WONDERS.

...may our hearts with gladness glow...

ALPHA L. BUNTAIN

*...when I think back to those nights
it is to the crunch of snow and to
the lights of the lanterns on it.*

| LAURIE LEE |

...there is still the same warm
feeling we had as children,
the same warmth that enfolds
our hearts and our homes.

JOAN WINMILL BROWN

We see new delights in

FAMILIAR TRADITIONS.

I smelt the rich scent of the heating spices; and admired the shining kitchen utensils, the polished clock, decked in holly, the silver mugs ranged on a tray ready to be filled...

| EMILY BRONTË |

Around the glowing hearth at night,
the harmless laugh and winter tale...

| JOHN CLARE |

I am reminded, during moments such as these, that the most important gifts I could ever receive are the ones that have already been given to me.

ANN MORROW

The festive lights and the gifts and the ornaments...
they are only a setting for the real jewel...

| NORMAN VINCENT PEALE |

There's magic in shared enjoyment,

IN TOGETHERNESS.

...laughter to cheer you, those

you love near you, and all

that your heart might desire.

IRISH BLESSING

Friends and family are reminders that

HOLIDAY WISHES COME TRUE.

| UNKNOWN |

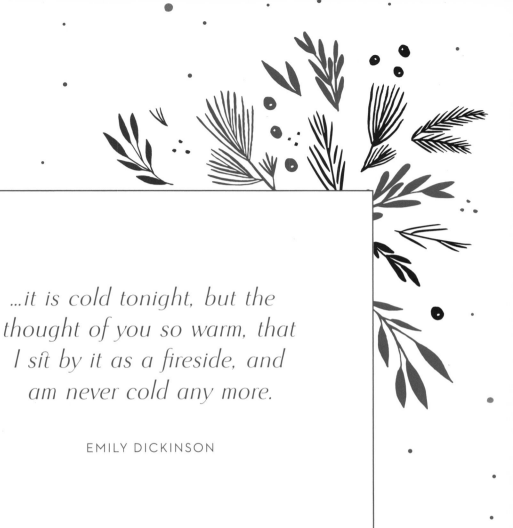

...it is cold tonight, but the thought of you so warm, that I sit by it as a fireside, and am never cold any more.

EMILY DICKINSON

Here's to all those near us,

AND THE LOVED ONES

who are far from us.

*In this tender season, rich
with memories, let us remember
all of those who have been
lights along our way...*

| DEBORAH GORDON COOPER |

Your abundance is not
measured by what you have,
it is created by what you share.

HEIDI CATHERINE CULBERTSON

Sing an old song.

SAY A BLESSING. CELEBRATE.

| JOANNE SELTZER |

This is the season of coming home.

| MAUREEN TOLMAN FLANNERY |

Our world is bright

WITH LOVE AND
LAUGHTER.

This door will open at a

touch to welcome every friend.

HENRY VAN DYKE JR.

Evenings we knew,
Happy as this;
Faces we miss,
Pleasant to see.

WILLIAM MAKEPEACE THACKERAY

When friends meet,

HEARTS WARM.

| PROVERB |

Kindness and generosity are

EVERYWHERE,

all around us.

Share your gifts with others,
pass along the cheer...

LIZZIE DE ARMOND

It isn't the size of the gift that matters,
but the size of the heart that gives it.

EILEEN ELIAS FREEMAN

...to your enemy, forgiveness.
To an opponent, tolerance.
To a friend, your heart...
To all, charity.

OREN ARNOLD

Scatter joy.

| RALPH WALDO EMERSON |

In this moment,

WE GLADLY SHARE
ALL WE HAVE.

May the holiday lights

always shine in your hearts...

DAWN M. MUELLER

Everybody's having fun. Look to the future now,

IT'S ONLY JUST BEGUN.

| NODDY HOLDER |

...a happy memory never wears out.

LIBBIE FUDIM

Here's to the most

WONDERFUL TIME
OF THE YEAR.

I will never be tired of the magic in the tinsel and lights of the tree.

| JEN MCCONNEL |

What a bright time...

JINGLE BELL ROCK, 1957 SONG

Like our memories, the ornaments are jumbled together with very little rhyme or reason, but they twinkle and catch your eye as you walk by...

| VICTORIA DEROSA |

*...I never can wish you a
greater happiness than this!*

| LOUISA MAY ALCOTT |

WE CARRY THIS
JOYFUL TIME
WITH US, ALWAYS.

May your coming year be

filled with magic and dreams...

NEIL GAIMAN

COMPENDIUM®
live inspired

*With special thanks to the
entire Compendium family.*

WRITTEN & COMPILED BY: RUTH AUSTIN

DESIGNED BY: JILL LABIENIEC

EDITED BY: AMELIA RIEDLER

ISBN: 978-1-946873-03-3

1st printing. Printed in China with soy and metallic inks.